MAGNET POWER!

Science Adventures with MAG-3000 the Origami Robot

by Thomas Kingsley Troupe

illustrated by Jamey Christoph

PICTURE WINDOW BOOKS
a capstone imprint

The spaceship's safety harnesses weren't working. The generator that powered the harnesses was missing a magnet. Everyone floated around as the ship drifted in space.

"I hope they send help soon," said the girl as she made the final paper fold.

The girl was finished with her origami robot. What else could she do to pass the time?

"Finished!" she said, holding the robot in the air.

"You are the heroic robot MAG-3000! HELP US, MAG!"

The computer inside MAG-3000's paper brain turned on. She opened her eyes and looked around at the floating people.

"MISSION: Restore power to the safety harnesses. Begin data collection now."

4

"Hey paper robot," a tiny voice squeaked. "what do you know about magnets?"

"Downloading data now," MAG said. Her robot body hummed. "Magnets are often made of metals such as steel, iron, cobalt, or nickel. Natural magnets called lodestones are sometimes found in the earth."

"Nice! I'm gordon."

"I am MAG-3000," MAG said.

"I fly around with my jetpack and fix things. The magnet that keeps the ship's electricity source working is missing. **can you help me find it?**"

"yes."

"perfect. without it, the family is left floating around. They can't fly to their vacation on planet Zeerk!"

Together he and MAG went to check out the problem.

POLES

A magnet's poles are attracted to opposite poles. A north pole will cling to a south pole, but a north pole will repel, or push away, another north pole. So it's true: Opposites attract!

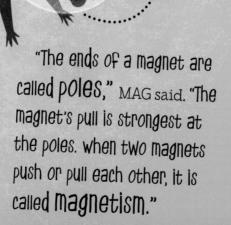

"A magnet has a north pole and a south pole."

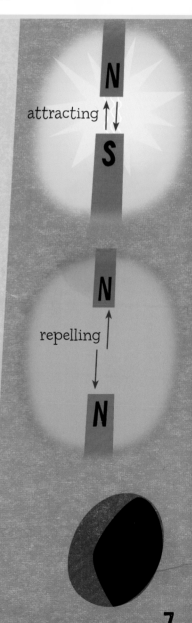

attracting

repelling

"A pole?"

"The ends of a magnet are called **poles**," MAG said. "The magnet's pull is strongest at the poles. When two magnets push or pull each other, it is called **magnetism**."

7

Gordon and MAG flew through a tunnel lined with wires and blinking lights.

"I still don't get it," Gordon said. "why does a magnet stick to all metals?"

"Correction. Magnets do not attract all metals. Stainless steel, brass, copper, aluminum, gold, and silver will not stick to magnets."

"Really?" Gordon said. "That's kind of weird."

"Tiny electrons within some metals move around, creating a **magnetic field.** The magnetic field draws other electrons toward it. This is why some metals stick together," MAG said.

"can we make magnets? I'd sure like to have one."

"yes," MAG said. "Try rubbing a metal paperclip on a magnet. Do it enough times, and it will become magnetized."

Gordon led MAG-3000 to the electric generator. The machine was bigger than anything MAG had ever seen.

"This is it. The machine that powers the safety harnesses. My plans show where the magnet should be."

"Magnets are used in many types of machines."

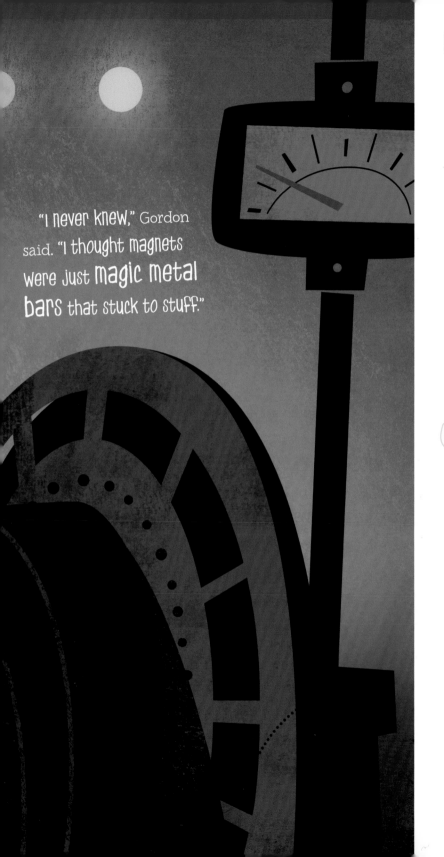

"I never knew," Gordon said. "I thought magnets were just **magic metal bars** that stuck to stuff."

speakers

refrigerators

computers

vacuum cleaners

Gordon showed MAG-3000 the generator up close and pointed at his blueprints.

"Okay, MAG, according to the plans, there should be a **magnet** in this part of the **generator**."

"My calculations say that without the magnet, the generator **won't function.** If the generator doesn't run, the safety harnesses won't work."

ENERGY

An electric generator uses a magnet to turn mechanical energy into electrical energy.

"I get it. The magnet helps the generator make electricity! But how are we going to find the magnet? It's gone!"

"Let's look and see."

"If we had another magnet," MAG beeped and whirred, "it might pull us to the missing magnet."

Gordon flew around and returned with two metal paperclips. They were huge in his small paws. He gave one of the paperclips to MAG.

"HOW about these things? DOES this kind of metal work on magnets?"

MAG floated past the generator and up into the air. The paperclip wobbled in her hands as a strong force pulled her across the room.

"I think we found the magnet. Up here!"

"It's pulling me too!"

"This magnet should fix the generator!"

MAG pulled, and Gordon pushed. Together they moved the magnet closer to the generator.

MAG slipped the magnet into place. Gordon
tightened it to keep it from falling out again.

"safety harnesses activated,"
a soft voice inside the ship
announced. Above them they
heard the family cheer.

GLOSSARY

attract—to pull something toward something else

blueprints—a plan for building

data—information or facts

electric generator—a machine that makes electricity by turning a magnet inside a coil of wire

harness—a device that straps one thing to another

lodestone—a stone containing iron that acts as a magnet

magnetic field—an area of moving electrical currents that affects other objects

magnetize—to cause an object to act like a magnet

mechanical energy—the energy an object has because of its motion or position

repel—to push apart

pole—one of the two ends of a magnet

READ MORE

Boothroyd, Jennifer. *Attract and Repel: A Look at Magnets.* Exploring Physical Science. Minneapolis: Lerner Publications, 2011.

Swanson, Jennifer. *The Attractive Truth about Magnetism.* LOL Physical Science. North Mankato, Minn.: Capstone Press, 2013.

Taylor-Butler, Christine. *Experiments with Magnets and Metals.* My Science Investigations. Chicago: Heinemann Library, 2012.

MAKE AN ORIGAMI ROBOT

MAG is one smart robot! Check out these instructions to make your own origami robot.

WHAT YOU'LL NEED

origami paper

WHAT YOU DO

Folds

- **Valley folds** are shown with a dashed line. One side of the paper is folded against the other like a book. A sharp fold is made by running your finger along the fold line.

- **Mountain folds** are shown with a white or pink dashed and dotted line. The paper should be folded sharply behind the model.

- **Squash folds** are formed by lifting one edge of a pocket. The pocket gets folded again so the spine gets flattened. The existing fold lines become new edges.

Arrows

single-pointed arrow: Fold the paper in the direction of the arrow.

double-pointed arrow: Fold the paper and then unfold it.

half-pointed arrow: Fold the paper behind.

looping arrow: Turn the paper over or turn it to a new position.

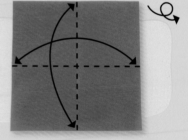

1. Start with the colored side of the paper face up. Valley fold the bottom edge to the top edge and unfold. Valley fold the left edge to the right edge and unfold. Turn the paper over.

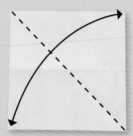

2. Valley fold the bottom-left corner to the top-right corner and unfold.

3. Valley fold the top-left corner down to the bottom-right corner.

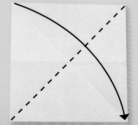

4. Squash fold by grabbing the paper's top-right corner. Pull the corner down to the left on the existing folds. Flatten the paper into a triangle.

5. Valley fold the bottom edges of the top layer to the center fold. Repeat this step on the back side of the model.

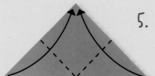

6. Valley fold both top points to the bottom point and unfold. Repeat this step on the back side of the model.

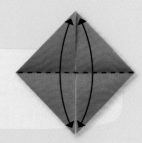

7. Squash fold both top flaps on the folds made in step 6. The flaps will flatten into squares. Repeat this step on the back side of the model.

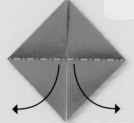

8. Valley fold both bottom-inside corners to the outside corners. Repeat this step on the back side of the model.

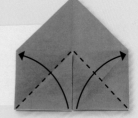

9. Mountain fold the left side of the top flap inside the model. Mountain fold the right side of the top flap inside the model. Repeat both of these folds on the back side of the model.

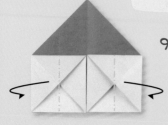

10. Valley fold the bottom point to the center edge. Repeat this step on the back side of the model.

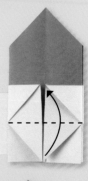

11. Pinch the triangles along the center edge of the model. Pull them out gently to form two arms. Then repeat this step on the back side of the model.

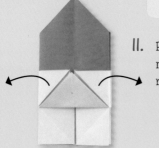

12. Have fun decorating your robot. Your MAG-3000 is complete!

INDEX

INTERNET SITES

FactHound offers a safe, fun way to find Internet sites related to this book. All of the sites on FactHound have been researched by our staff.

Here's all you do:

Visit www.facthound.com

Type in this code: 9781404879720

Check out projects, games and lots more at
www.capstonekids.com

Read all the books in the series:

Diggin' Dirt: Science Adventures with Kitanai the Origami Dog

Let's Rock!: Science Adventures with Rudie the Origami Dinosaur

Magnet Power!: Science Adventures with MAG-3000 the Origami Robot

Plant Parts Smarts: Science Adventures with Charlie the Origami Bee

Thanks to our advisers for their expertise, research, and advice:
Paul Ohmann, PhD, Associate Professor and Chair of Physics
University of St. Thomas

Terry Flaherty, PhD, Professor of English
Minnesota State University, Mankato

Editor: Shelly Lyons
Designer: Ashlee Suker
Art Director: Nathan Gassman
Production Specialist: Eric Manske
The illustrations in this book were created digitally.

Picture Window Books are published by Capstone,
1710 Roe Crest Drive, North Mankato, Minnesota 56003
www.capstonepub.com

Library of Congress Cataloging-in-Publication Data
Troupe, Thomas Kingsley.
Magnet power! : science adventures with MAG-3000
the origami robot / by Thomas Kingsley Troupe ;
illustrated by Jamey Christoph.
pages cm. — (Origami science adventures)
Audience: K to grade 3
ISBN 978-1-4048-7972-0 (library binding)
ISBN 978-1-4048-8070-2 (paperback)
ISBN 978-1-4795-0002-4 (eBook PDF)
1. Magnetics—Juvenile literature. 2. Magnets—Juvenile literature.
3. Origami—Juvenile literature. I. Christoph, James, illustrator.
II. Title.
QC757.5.T76 2013
538—dc23   2012029513

Photo credits:
Digital illustrations include royalty-free images from Shutterstock.
Capstone Studio: Karon Dubke, 22-23; Shutterstock: ifong, 11 (laptop),
Photoseeker, 11 (vacuum cleaner), shutswis, 11 (speakers), Todd
Taulman, 11 (refrigerator)

Printed in the United States of America in Brainerd, Minnesota.
092012   006938BANGS13